Joseph M. Brown

The Mountain Campaigns in Georgia

Joseph M. Brown

The Mountain Campaigns in Georgia

ISBN/EAN: 9783743344983

Manufactured in Europe, USA, Canada, Australia, Japa

Cover: Foto ©ninafisch / pixelio.de

Manufactured and distributed by brebook publishing software
(www.brebook.com)

Joseph M. Brown

The Mountain Campaigns in Georgia

MOUNTAIN CAMPAIGNS

IN GEORGIA

OF

WAR SCENES ON THE W. & A.

. . .

ACT-PRINTING WORKS OF MATTHEWS, NORTHRUP & CO., BUFFALO, N. Y.

THE OPINIONS OF

GEN. WM. T. SHERMAN AND GEN. JOSEPH E. JOHNSTON

ABOUT THE

"*Mountain Campaigns in Georgia, or War Scenes on the W. & A.*"

FROM GEN. W. T. SHERMAN.

912 GARRISON AVENUE,
ST. LOUIS, MO., Jan. 18, 1886.

JOS. M. BROWN, ESQ.
Western & Atlantic R. R., Atlanta, Ga.

MY DEAR SIR: I beg to acknowledge receipt of your letter of January 14th, with the embellished pamphlet entitled "THE MOUNTAIN CAMPAIGNS IN GEORGIA," and take great pleasure in complimenting you on having made so condensed and valuable a souvenir of the old State Railroad from Chattanooga to Atlanta.

The maps are admirable, the illustrations are characteristic, and the text as near the truth as can be compressed in so small a space. I am willing to endorse what you record — that the Atlanta Campaign of 1864 would have been impossible without this road, that all our battles were fought for its possession, and that the Western & Atlantic Railroad of Georgia "should be the pride of every true American," because, "by reason of its existence the Union was saved."

I infer you have prepared this costly pamphlet to induce travel by this route, and I will add that the scenery will fully repay every lover of nature's beauty and sublimity; that every foot of it should be sacred ground, because it was once moistened by patriotic blood; and that over a hundred miles of it was fought a continuous battle of one hundred and twenty days, during which, day and night, were heard the continuous boom of cannon and the sharp crack of the rifle.

I sincerely wish for you, and all like you, all success, prosperity and happiness, in these days of peace, made possible by the deadly struggles between Chattanooga and Atlanta in the summer of 1864.
With great respect, your friend,

W. T. SHERMAN.

FROM GEN. JOSEPH E. JOHNSTON.

WASHINGTON, D. C., Jan. 18, 1886.

JOS. M. BROWN, ESQ.

MY DEAR SIR: Your letter of the 14th, and the beautiful "WAR SCENES" that came by the same mail, were received this morning, and I thank you for them most cordially, not only for the pleasure they have already given me, but because you put before the public an excellent historical sketch in so attractive a form as to secure for operations most interesting to me the attention of our Southern people. I have seen no publication relating to the war so attractive in style and appearance.

With friendly regards to your brother, I am,

Yours very truly,

J. E. JOHNSTON.

BATTLE OF KENNESAW MOUNTAIN.
On the line of the Western & Atlantic Railroad, near Marietta, Ga.

GEN. W. T. SHERMAN.

All Colored People

THAT WANT TO

GO TO KANSAS,

On September 5th, 1877,

Can do so for $5.00

IMMIGRATION

WHEREAS, We, the colored people of Lexington, Ky., knowing that there is an abundance of choice lands now belonging to the Government, have assembled ourselves together for the purpose of locating on said lands. Therefore,

Be it RESOLVED, That we do now organize ourselves into a Colony, as soon as — Any person wishing to become a member of this Colony can do so by paying the sum of one dollar ($1.00), and this money is to be paid by the first of September, ... installments of twenty-five cents at a time, or otherwise as may be desired.

RESOLVED, That this Colony has agreed to consolidate itself with the Nicodemus Towns, Solomon Valley, Graham County, Kansas, and can only do so by securing the vacant lands now in their midst, which costs $5.00.

RESOLVED, That this Colony shall consist of seven officers—President, Vice-President, Secretary, Treasurer, and three Trustees. President—M. M. Bell; Vice-President —Isaac Talbott; Secretary—W. J. Niles; Treasurer—Daniel Clarke; Trustees—Jerry Lee, William Jones, and Abner Webster.

RESOLVED, That this Colony shall have from one to two hundred militia, more or less, as the case may require, to keep peace and order, and any member failing to pay in his dues, as aforesaid, or failing to comply with the above rules in any particular, will not be recognized or protected by the Colony.

·PREFACE·

THE AUTHORITIES principally consulted in preparing the text of this publication are "Johnston's Narrative," "Sherman's Memoirs," Cox's "Atlanta," and magazine articles by General S. G. French, and Major Geo. S. Storrs, and the daily files of the *Atlanta Intelligencer*, issued during the years of 1863 and 1864.

The cuts, which were prepared by Mr. A. R. Waud, who personally visited all of the battlefields depicted, and by Messrs. T. de Thulstrup and Joseph Fleming, have been drawn with scrupulous regard to historic accuracy, as well as artistic skill, and engraved by Matthews, Northrup & Co., of Buffalo, N. Y. The maps, drawn and engraved by Matthews, Northrup & Co., of Buffalo, N. Y., are based on the authority of Sherman's maps of the Atlanta campaign, with corrections when proper, and speak for themselves as models of their kind.

If there be errors of fact, or aught else subject to criticism herein, it is hoped that lenient judgment will be passed, when it is taken into consideration that the matter has been prepared during only such time as could be snatched from that required for supervision over the freight and passenger traffic of a railroad, the most of whose business is competitive.

THE MOUNTAIN CAMPAIGNS IN GEORGIA:

or War Scenes on the W. & A.

IN NONE of the campaigns of the gigantic "War between the States" was there a more notable display of adroit, wary, far-reaching strategic genius, and prudent, patient, watchful care on the part of the great commanders; of zealous, skillful and fearless leadership by their field officers, or of more heroic bravery, fortitude and cheerful endurance by the soldiery, than in those of 1863 and 1864, during which the world became familiar with the names of Chickamauga, Missionary Ridge, Ringgold, Rocky Face, Dalton, Resaca, Allatoona, Kennesaw Mountain and Atlanta.

Grant, Sherman, Sheridan, Rosecrans, Thomas, McPherson, Schofield, Hooker, Corse, Blair, Harker, Kilpatrick, Stoneman, and a half score of others scarcely less famous, on some or all of these fields directed and led the hundred thousand and upwards, who followed the "bright starry banner" of the Union; while Bragg, and afterwards Johnston, with Hardee, Hood, Polk, Longstreet, Cleburne, Breckenridge, Buckner, Forrest, French, Walthall and Wheeler, with brother-chieftains as valiant and devoted, showed that the South had sent her brainiest and bravest to endeavor, with their fifty thousand men, to stem the tide of invasion which was rolling through Georgia, the Keystone State of the Confederacy, against Atlanta, which was then, as now, considered the "Heart of the South."

To the essayist, wishing to immortalize with his pen the great deeds of great men, here is opened one of History's favorite chapters; to the artist, eager to depict the romantic and picturesque in warfare, here, too, is displayed the scenery which thrills the emotions; while to the patriot, who delights to speak of the achievements of men who dared face death for their country, their cause and their flag, here is shown the theatre of their toils and their glory.

With these few reflections, let us now turn immediately to the record of the stirring events between Chattanooga, Kennesaw Mountain and Atlanta, which twenty-two years ago were the cynosure of the eyes of the civilized world.

Early in September, 1863, General Rosecrans succeeded in capturing Bridgeport, Ala., thus securing a crossing over the Tennessee River.

He then pushed Thomas and McCook, with their corps, across Sand Mountain and Lookout Mountain, into Georgia, and obtained possession of the passes leading into McLemore's Cove, from which West Chickamauga Creek flows northeastward, and, joining the main Chickamauga, empties into the Tennessee River just east of Chattanooga.

GEN. WM. T. SHERMAN

This made their position in Chattanooga a perilous one for the Confederates, inasmuch as Rosecrans's movements, if carried out successfully, would have secured for him possession of Dalton and Rome, and thus broken Bragg's communications with Atlanta, and forced him to have retreated through East Tennessee, and left Georgia at the mercy of the Federal arms.

As one of the Southern newspapers of that day said, of the game of military chess which was then being played, "The enemy attacked with his Knight both our Queen, Atlanta, and our Castle, Chattanooga. Did it require a moment to decide what should be the move?"

Bragg accordingly evacuated Chattanooga on September 7, 1863, and retired to a position between Ringgold and Graysville, on the Western & Atlantic Railroad, and La Fayette, in Walker county, west of the railroad. His main army was posted along the road leading from Gordon's Mill to La Fayette, facing the passes through which Rosecrans was about to make his entrance into McLemore's Cove.

On the 9th of September, the Federal army occupied Chattanooga. During the next ten days there was almost daily skirmishing, and, on some occasions, vigorous fighting, at various points between Ringgold and La Fayette. There was also a sharp cavalry contest at Catoosa Springs, near the Western & Atlantic Railroad, September 11th, which resulted in the retreat of the Confederates to Tunnel Hill, where they received re-enforcements. At Ringgold a heavy cavalry fight also ensued on September 11th. The Confederates were at first driven into the town; but here rallied, and, under General Forrest, repulsed the Federals, and drove them off in disorder.

The two armies were maneuvering for position—Rosecrans being resolved to hold Bragg off, until he could secure such a disposition of his own as was essential to success;

while Bragg, on the contrary, was determined to force an engagement at the earliest attainable date, with the object of crushing Rosecrans's army, in a general engagement, if it were at all possible.

It is not practicable, in our limited space, to give scarcely any of these movements in detail.

On the 18th of September was fired the first gun of what is known as the great battle of Chickamauga. The position of the two armies that morning, in brief, was as follows:

Rosecrans occupied the northwest bank of West Chickamauga Creek, his line extending along its sinuous course for a dozen miles or more, guarding all the fords, bridges, or other places of transit, for the purpose of preventing a crossing by the Confederate army.

The Confederates were on the southeast side of the creek, which is very muddy and generally very deep; and Bragg's idea was to force his way over, at various points, and fight the battle on the Chattanooga side of the creek.

At Reed's Bridge, in Catoosa county, Ga., some seven miles west of Ringgold, a detachment of Michigan cavalry was stationed, with orders to prevent any advance by the Confederates. Having been there for a day or more, their commander determined, that morning, to send about 200 mounted men across the bridge, for the purpose of making a reconnoissance, and developing the Confederate position. At the same time he ordered that the planks be loosened, so that, when the cavalry returned, these could be dropped into the creek, and the bridge thus practically destroyed. The detachment crossed the stream, as ordered, and the work of loosening the planks was commenced by the others.

The scouting party, however, had scarcely begun deploying on the east side of the creek before the Confederates, who had been watching them some couple of hundred yards distant, at the edge of the woods on the summit of the elevation rising from the bridge, opened fire, from a couple of pieces of artillery. The very first discharge secured the range of the bridge, and a bombshell exploding upon it, knocked up some of the planks,

GEN. JOSEPH E. JOHNSTON.

and killed one man, and wounded two others. Almost at the same instant a volley of musketry was fired from the same position.

The work of destruction of the bridge by the Federals instantly ceased, and there was a stampede for cover to the forest near by. The detachment of cavalry on the east bank, seeing the folly of attempting to cross the bridge under a raking fire, galloped northeastward, down the creek, endeavoring to find some other crossing place. After going about a mile and a half and finding no regular ford, they swam their horses through the stream, and thus escaped.

In the meantime, the Confederates charged across the bridge, dispersed the cavalry, and immediately turned downward, towards Alexander's Bridge, about one mile and a half distant, and, after quite a struggle, possession of this was also secured.

Later on, during the day, crossing was effected at several other points. Accordingly, the next morning found Bragg's army, in line of battle, on the northwest side of West Chickamauga Creek.

The struggle then began, which continued with such desperate fury, and resulted in such distressing carnage to both sides, during the next three days.

Bragg's object seems to have been to crush Rosecrans's left wing, and secure possession of the road leading through Missionary Ridge, via Rossville, to Chattanooga.

The result of the battle is well known. Rosecrans's army was routed and driven back to Chattanooga; and, but for the stand which General Thomas took, on Snodgrass Hill, and his heroic defence of that position, and the check which he gave to the Confederates at that point, the defeat of Rosecrans would have been a crushing one, and the sweep of the Confederate advance may have extended back to Kentucky, and have almost changed the fate of the war. "But great battles are fought behind the stars."

The struggle at Snodgrass Hill was desperate and bloody in the extreme, and was characterized as being "unquestionably one of the most terrific musketry duels ever witnessed"; but Thomas, having been re-enforced by Granger and Steadman, who had moved, without orders, to join him, held this position until all the rest of the Federal line of battle had been routed, and only retreated on the evening of the 20th, under orders from General Rosecrans himself.

The total losses sustained have never been definitely ascertained; but it is generally estimated that there were over 26,000 men killed and wounded in the two armies, during these bloody three days, on and near the banks of the Chickamauga, or "River of Death," as the Indians had prophetically named it.

Among the killed was the Federal General Lytle, the author of the famous and beautiful poem, "I am dying, Egypt, dying."

Of his death, the *Nashville Union*, a few days after the battle, said:

"He, with hundreds of his loyal soldiers, has consecrated with his life-blood the soil of Georgia to the Republic. Let us solemnly pledge ourselves that the State thus baptized by blood so dear shall never pass from the possession of the Union. It is our heritage and the heritage of our children forever, signed to us in the name of freedom and sealed with the blood of patriots."

The Confederates captured 8,000 prisoners, 51 cannon, over 15,000 stand of small arms, about 40 standards, and an enormous amount of army stores.

The battle-field was principally in a level, thickly-wooded plain, where it was hard to use artillery with much effect, and where the movements of large bodies of troops were veiled in obscurity.

It is stated that there were numerous instances of where portions of one army's line were driven back by its enemy, and these, in turn, would soon find themselves caught by a cross-fire, or almost surrounded by a counter successful movement by the other side.

THE FIRST GUN AT CHICKAMAUGA.
September 18, 1863.
The Confederates opening fire upon the Federal cavalry, who had begun the destruction of Reed's Bridge.

The strength of Rosecrans's army, during the three days' struggle, was 64,302 men. Bragg opened with 33,585 the first day; but, during the second, was re-enforced by Longstreet's corps, which had just arrived from Virginia, and which made his total force engaged 47,321.

Longstreet's troops arrived via the Western & Atlantic Railroad, and deployed from the trains at Ringgold and Greenwood, just below, and hurried into the midst of the fray.

As the result of this battle, the Federal army was driven back into Chattanooga; and the Confederates occupied Missionary Ridge and Lookout Mountain, from which latter they could overlook Chattanooga, and by the possession of which they were enabled to break Rosecrans's communications by rail with Nashville. They also re-occupied Bridgeport.

Thus matters continued for two months, during which there was great suffering among the Federal soldiery, in Chattanooga, on account of the difficulty in getting provisions, stores, etc., across the country in wagons.

By the end of that time, however, the Union army had been very largely re-enforced, and General Grant had come to Chattanooga and taken personal command. He also had with him Generals Sherman, Sheridan, Thomas, McPherson, Hooker, and other leaders of national reputation for marked ability.

In the meantime, Bragg had sent Longstreet's corps to Knoxville, for the purpose of reducing that point, and repossessing East Tennessee.

This movement had weakened his numbers at Chattanooga very materially; so that when, on the morning of November 24, 1863, General Grant made his attack upon Bragg, with about 65,000 of the best-equipped and bravest soldiers in America, the latter confronted him with a line extending about seven miles from the crest of Lookout Mountain, across the gap between that and Missionary Ridge, and thence along the summit of Missionary Ridge, almost to the present Boyce Station, on the Western & Atlantic Railroad, with a total force of scarcely more than 35,000 men.

During the night of November 24th, Hooker's corps clambered through the clouds, concealing its movements, up the sides of Lookout Mountain, which was held by Walthall's brigade of Confederates.

The Confederate force, during the early portion of the night, consisted of 1,489 men. At about midnight they received re-enforcements of about 600 more. The fight continued fiercely, amid the thick mists which completely enveloped the steep and craggy heights, until about two o'clock A. M. of November 25th, when the mountain was abandoned by the Confederates, who retired, in comparatively good order, down its sides across Chattanooga Creek Valley to Missionary Ridge. Several hundred of them, however, were cut off and captured. During the latter part of the fight the clouds drifted from the mountain side, exposing the majestic panorama to the eyes of the Confederates on Missionary Ridge. The view from the Ridge is said to have been magnificently grand, the flashings and blaze of musketry and artillery being almost incessant, while, like distant angry thunder, the reverberations rolled far across the hills and down the long valleys.

On the morning of the 25th, the combat began all along the line for about a half a dozen miles. The evolutions of the Federal army, on the plain below, were described by the Confederates as being as regular as upon dress parade. The assault was impetuous; but for several hours it appeared as if the Confederates would hold ths position. Sherman's attack upon the Confederate right met a masterly repulse at the hands of the lion-hearted Cleburne. The assault was renewed with desperate energy; but again Cleburne held his own, against fearful odds, hurling back the attacking columns with great loss, and capturing seven stands of colors. General Hardee, who commanded the Confederate right wing, was at all points along his front as the terrific struggle progressed. His troops had

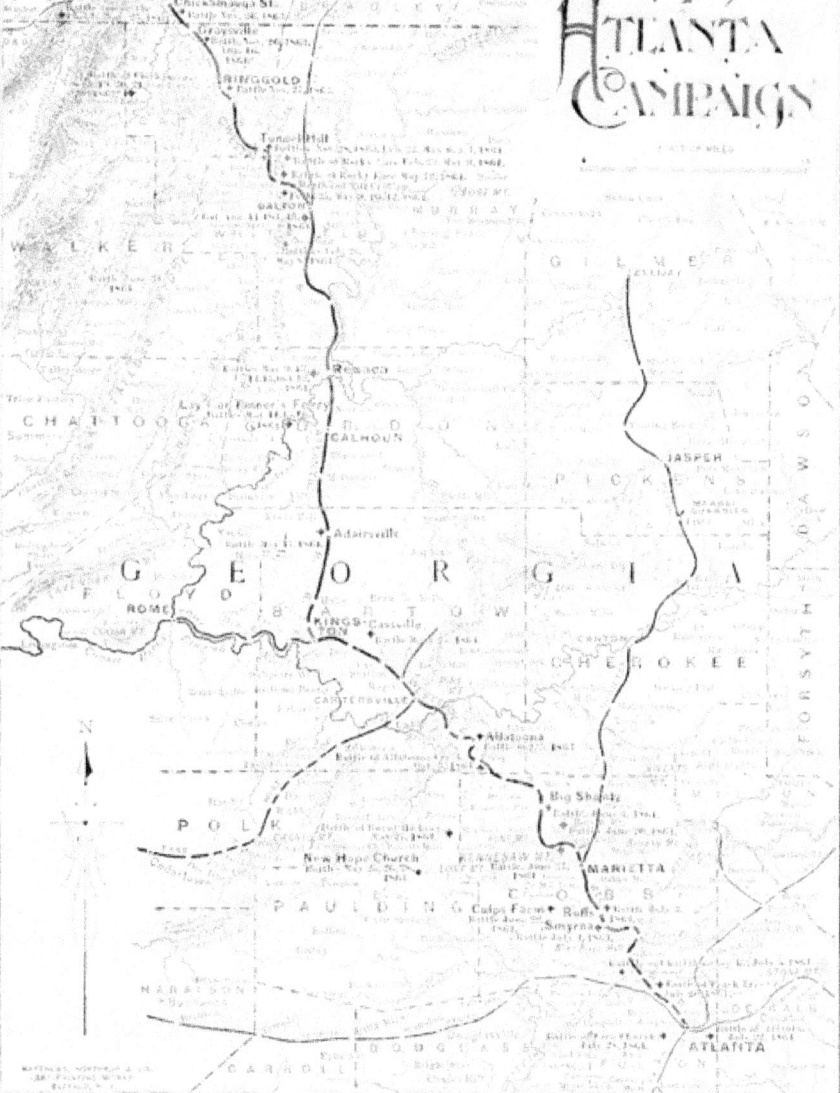

Map of the
ATLANTA
CAMPAIGN

CHATTANOOGA

T E N N.

Chickamauga Sta.

Graysville

RINGGOLD

Tunnel Hill

DALTON

W A L K E R

M U R R A Y

G I L M E R

Resaca

CHATTOOGA

CALHOUN

JASPER

P I C K E N S

D A W S O N

Adairsville

G E O R G I A

ROME

B A R T O W

KINGS-Cassville
TON

C H E R O K E E

F O R S Y T H

CARTERSVILLE

N

Allatoona

P O L K

Big Shanty

New Hope Church

KENESAW MT.

MARIETTA

C O B B

P A U L D I N G

Culps Farm
Ruffs

Smyrna

N A R A L S O N

D O U G L A S S

ATLANTA

CARROLL

repulsed the Federal attack upon them wherever made, and were cheering for victory at the very moment Grant's columns were breaking through the Confederate left center, and rending the air with their enthusiastic shouts. General Hardee discovering the catastrophe, galloped to his left, and formed Jackson's and Moore's brigades across the ridge, and checked the Federals on his flank, and, with Cheatham's division, held this till dark, when he drew off his entire command, in good order and without the loss of a single gun in any of his batteries.

Soon after the Confederate center was broken, at about four P. M., the entire line except the right gave way; and the result was a disastrous rout of Bragg's army, with a loss of about 40 pieces of cannon, 6,000 prisoners, and 3,400 killed and wounded. The loss of the Federal army in killed and wounded was 5,286 men, besides 337 missing.

The next day there was a very spirited conflict near Chickamauga Station, on the Western & Atlantic Railroad. The Confederates were partially intrenched, but soon abandoned the position.

That evening the head of Sherman's columns encountered the rear-guard of Bragg's retreating army near Graysville, also a station on the railroad. The fight was quite sharp; but a dark night closed upon the combatants, and, during the night, the Confederates retired.[*]

The next day Hooker, rapidly pursuing, found General Cleburne, with his and a portion of Bate's divisions, at Ringgold. Cleburne had stationed his forces on the ridge just southeast of Ringgold, and in the ravine by which the Western & Atlantic Railroad passes through it. The Confederates had several pieces of artillery on the crest of the ridge, immediately east of the town, and also a masked battery in the ravine. The Federal head of column passed this latter; but suddenly, in this mountain pass, discovered the Confederate intrenchments in front, from which a destructive fire was opened upon them. As they were thus thrown into disorder, the masked battery opened upon their flank; and they were compelled to retire precipitately to the plain, in which the town is located.

They here formed and made a determined attack upon the Confederates at all points. The fighting in the ravine through which the railroad runs, and in the counter ravine at the northern end of the short ridge extending from the pass, several hundred yards parallel to the railroad, was very desperate and bloody. The assaulting columns made some progress up the sides of the ridge, when the fire from the Confederate line became so destructive, and the rolling of huge rocks down the mountain slope threw the assailants into such confusion, and inflicted such loss, that they were compelled to give over the attack. Hooker's forces then fell back from the town, burning it as they departed.

This vigorous resistance, on Cleburne's part, temporarily checked the pursuit of Bragg's army, and saved a very large wagon train, which had been parked at Catoosa Station, and which the Confederates were preparing to burn, in the event that Cleburne was driven back from Ringgold.

---

[*] Graysville was also the scene of a hot fight between Wheeler's Confederate cavalry and the Federals, on August 16th of the same year. This was during the siege of Atlanta, and Hood had sent Wheeler to raid Sherman's communications.

One of the relics of this bloody struggle is the Jobe house, which stands in the northern end of the pass, on the west side of the railroad.

On the day of the battle, some of Hooker's men took shelter in this, and, from the windows and doors, maintained a hot fire upon the Confederates on the ridge and in the pass. The latter in return kept a storm of bullets pouring upon the house, the numerous marks of which are still plainly visible.

The next day, the Confederates, who had retired to Tunnel Hill, were assailed by the Federal forces with a courage almost amounting, it is said, to rashness; but they held the position, and the Federals then retired to Ringgold, and afterwards to Chattanooga, tearing up the railroad behind them, thus leaving the beautiful Chickamauga Valley as a sort of neutral zone between the hostile forces.

From that date, there was comparative quiet between the two armies for nearly three months; but, on the 23d of February, 1864, the Federals made a movement in heavy force, with the intention of securing possession of Dalton, if possible, while the Confederate army was weakened by the absence of Hood's corps, consisting of Cheatham's, Cleburne's and Walker's divisions, which had been sent to Mississippi to re-enforce General Polk.

Just here it is proper to state that, during the winter, General Bragg had been relieved, at his own request, from the command of the Confederate army of Tennessee, and the Richmond government, in compliance with almost the open demand of Southern popular opinion, had appointed General Joseph E. Johnston to succeed him, and he had proceeded to Dalton and assumed command December 27, 1863.

Later on, General Grant had been appointed Lieutenant-General of the armies of the United States, and had transferred his head-quarters to Virginia; and had designated General Wm. T. Sherman as his successor over the Department of the Mississippi, which included Tennessee and Georgia. General Sherman entered upon his duties March 18, 1864, General Thomas having had temporary charge of the Federal forces at Chattanooga, after General Grant proceeded east, just as General Hardee had temporarily commanded the Confederate army at Dalton, after General Bragg's retirement.

The Federal columns, February 23d, united in front of Ringgold, and advancing, attacked the Confederate cavalry, and, after a sharp fight, drove it from the village of Tunnel Hill to the heights beyond; but were here checked by the artillery fire, and fell back.

The next day, the Federal army advanced in three columns, and compelled the Confederates to retire. The latter took position in Crow Valley (lying east of Rocky Face Ridge and north of Mill Creek Gap). The Federals encamped in the valley immediately west of the pass through which the railroad runs.

On the morning of the 25th, the Federal skirmishers engaged Stewart's and Breckenridge's divisions in Mill Creek Gap, and desultory firing was maintained throughout the day. This culminated in a determined but unsuccessful attempt to storm the position that afternoon.

During the same afternoon a very obstinate fight took place between the two armies, the divisions of Davis and Johnson attempting to drive the Confederates from Mill Creek Gap, while Cruft's and Baird's divisions, with Long's cavalry, attacked five brigades of Hindman's and Stevenson's divisions, east of Rocky Face Ridge, with the intention of defeating these, if possible, and then attacking in the rear the Confederate force which was holding Mill Creek Gap against Davis and Johnson; but at night the Federals gave over the attempt and fell back.

During this same day, the Confederate guard, posted in Dug Gap, west of Dalton, was driven from it by a regiment of Federal mounted infantry; but the next morning Granberry's Texas brigade made an impetuous charge, and recaptured the position.

General Johnston says that in this engagement, " The Federal army had four divisions and six regiments—probably at least seventeen brigades; it encountered seven Confederate brigades on the 25th, and eleven on the 26th."

General Thomas's report of these operations sustains General Johnston's estimate of the Federal force.

There was no other engagement between the two armies, until Sherman opened the " Atlanta Campaign," during the first week in May, 1864.

On the 2d day of this month, the Federals made a close reconnoissance of the Confederate outpost at Tunnel Hill, under the protection of a strong body of infantry, cavalry and artillery. They also began repairing the Western & Atlantic Railroad, between Chattanooga and Ringgold, which had been torn up the previous winter.

It may be here remarked that the Western & Atlantic Railroad was the means of securing the fall of Atlanta, and, therefore, to a great degree, the overthrow of the Southern Confederacy. It was Sherman's only channel for supplies for his immense army, and, during the campaign, he hugged it with a tenacity which showed that he considered it indispensable to success. His flank movement through Snake Creek Gap was to gain possession of it at Resaca, in the rear of Johnston at Dalton; his move against Calhoun, south of Resaca, via Lay's Ferry, had the same end in view. Such, likewise, was his object, indirectly, in the skillfully-planned and masterly march and struggles about New Hope Church, and such was his immediate aim in the movement southwest of Marietta, after the failure of his grand and heroic assault upon Kennesaw Mountain.

One hundred and forty-five car-loads per day of supplies were needed for the subsistence of his army, during the campaign, and over this railroad they were transported from Chattanooga.

To insure its preservation, as he progressed farther and farther southward, he placed garrisons to protect each bridge.

Johnston, too, was fully alive to the supreme importance of this line to both armies, and, while his constant endeavor was to protect it behind him, it was also his most ardent desire to find some means for breaking it in Sherman's rear; and thus forcing upon the latter the alternative of retreat or starvation. To this end he and the Governor of Georgia made the strongest appeals to the Richmond government for Forrest's cavalry to be brought from Mississippi and kept actively at the work of destruction upon the railroad bridges, etc.; using the argument that it was better to take the risk of Federal raids in northern Mississippi than to lose the opportunity of forcing into disastrous retreat the invading army which was driving its advance like a wedge of steel into the very heart of the Confederacy.

These entreaties, however, were without success, and the Western & Atlantic Railroad, despite Sherman's constant apprehensions of the realization of Johnston's wish, remained the chief means by which the invasion was sustained, and crowned with the fall of Atlanta.

As a prominent Federal authority said, after the war, to a Western & Atlantic official, "The Union element cannot be too thankful for the fact that your road was in existence."

"Then," was the remark, "the W. & A. road should be the pride of every true American, if by reason of its existence the Union was saved."

At the date of the opening of the great Atlanta Campaign, Sherman had a total force of 98,797 men and 254 cannon, divided as follows: Army of the Cumberland, under Major-General Thomas, 60,773 men, and 130 field guns; Army of the Tennessee, under Major-General McPherson, 24,465 men, and 96 guns; Army of the Ohio, under Major-General Schofield, 13,559 men, and 28 guns. These were further subdivided into 88,188 infantry, 4,460 artillerymen, and 6,149 cavalry.

Johnston had 42,856 men and 120 cannon; the men being divided as follows: infantry 37,652, artillerists 2,812, and cavalry 2,392. He says of his cannon, however, that only about one half of them were effective for service, because of the bad condition of the horses, by reason of the scarcity of food during the winter. Within a few days Sherman was re-enforced by about 14,000 cavalry, which swelled his total effective force to 112,819 men. All of these figures are official.

Added to these were the re-enforcements which the two armies received during the campaign, which were as follows: By Sherman, Blair's corps, 9,000 men at Acworth, June 8th, besides "new regiments and furloughed men" not enumerated; by Johnston, Canty's division of 3,000 at Resaca, May 9th, Loring's of 5,000, at the same point, May 11th, and French's of 4,000, at Cassville, on May 18th — these three comprising Polk's corps — also Martin's division of cavalry, 3,500, May 9th, Jackson's division of cavalry, 3,900, at Adairsville, May 17th, and Quarles's brigade of 2,200, at New Hope Church, May 26th.

While fighting around Kennesaw Mountain, General Johnston also received re-enforcements of over 3,000 Georgia militia, which Governor Joseph E. Brown, the "War Governor" of Georgia, placed at his disposal.

During the entire campaign, Governor Brown, now United States Senator from Georgia, and President of the Western & Atlantic Railroad Company, very zealously and energetically seconded General Johnston in every attempt to check and repel Sherman's invasion of the State.

The highest number of men which Johnston had at any time was 59,248, at Kennesaw Mountain.

Of the opening of this campaign, General Johnston says:

"On the 5th, the Confederate troops were formed to receive the enemy: Stewart's and Bate's divisions, in Mill Creek Gap, in which they had constructed some slight defensive works—the former on the right of the stream, Cheatham's on Stewart's right, occupying about a mile of the crest of the mountain; Walker's in reserve; Stevenson's across Crow Valley; its left joining Cheatham's right, on the crest of the mountain; Hindman's, on the right of Stevenson's; and Cleburne's, immediately in front of Dalton, and behind Mill Creek, facing towards Cleveland.

"On the same day the Federal army was formed in order of battle, three miles in front of Tunnel Hill, and in that position skirmished with our advanced guard until dark. It was employed all of the next in selecting and occupying a position just beyond the range of the field-pieces of the Confederate advanced guard, on which it halted for the night. * * *

"At day-break, on the 7th, the Federal army moved forward, annoyed and delayed in its advance by dismounted Confederate cavalry firing upon it from the cover of successive lines of very slight entrenchments, prepared the day before. Its progress was so slow, that the Confederates were not driven from Tunnel Hill until eleven o'clock A. M., nor to Mill Creek Gap until three P. M. In the afternoon the Federal army placed itself in front of the Confederate line, its right a little south of Mill Creek Gap, and its left near the Cleveland road."—(JOHNSTON'S NARRATIVE, pages 304, 305.)

General Sherman says of Johnston's position:

"From Tunnel Hill, I could look into the gorge by which the railroad passed through a straight and well-defined range of mountains, presenting sharp palisade faces, and known as 'Rocky Face.' The gorge itself was called the 'Buzzard Roost.' We could plainly see the enemy in this gorge and behind it, and Mill Creek which formed the gorge, flowing toward Dalton, had been dammed up, making a sort of irregular lake, filling the road, thereby obstructing it, and the enemy's batteries crowned the cliffs on either side."—(MEMOIRS, Vol. II., page 32.)

About four o'clock the next day, Geary's division of Hooker's corps assailed the Confederate outpost in Dug Gap; but two small regiments of Reynolds's Arkansas brigade, under the command of Colonel Williamson, held the position, until they were joined by Grigsby's Kentuckians.

The constant firing indicated a serious attack; so much so that Lieutenant-General Hardee hastened to take personal charge of the defence. The Federals were repulsed at this point, and at Mill Creek Gap, and likewise in their attack upon the Confederate position on the crest of the mountain, about a mile and a half north of the gap.

BATTLE OF RESACA, GA.

On the line of the Western & Atlantic Railroad.

May 15, 1864.

The assault against Gen. Hindman's position by a portion of the Army of the Cumberland.

General J. D. Cox, of Sherman's army, thus refers to this attempt on Dug Gap:

"Geary's division of the Twentieth Corps made a strong effort to carry the summit of Rocky Face at Dug Gap, but were foiled by the same physical difficulties which baffled all other attempts along this palisaded ridge. The skirmishers advanced, scrambling over the rocks and through the undergrowth, till, already blown and nearly exhausted, they found themselves facing a perpendicular wall with only cliffs and crevices leading up through it, the narrow roadway which had been their guide being strongly held by the enemy and intrenched. A gallant effort was made to reach the crest, but the smaller force of Confederates was led by General Hardee in person, and held their natural fortress."—("ATLANTA," page 35.)

On the 9th, another attempt, more vigorous and by a larger force, was made upon the outposts upon the crest of Rocky Face Ridge. This attack was led by Harker's brigade of Newton's division (Fourth Corps), supported by the rest of the division, and by Judah's division of the Army of the Ohio. The Federals were driven back with loss, after making five assaults.

Of this struggle, General Cox thus writes:

"The view of the combat above was an exciting one. The line of blue coats could be seen among the rocks, nearly at right angles with the line of the ridge, the men at the top in *silhouette* against the sky, close up to the Confederate trenches, where their charges were met with a line of fire, before which they recoiled, only to renew the effort, till it became apparent even to the most daring that it was useless to lead men against such barriers."—("ATLANTA," pages 37, 38.)

Similar assaults were also made upon Stewart's and Bate's divisions in Mill Creek Gap; but the Confederates maintained their position.

On this same day quite an important fight occurred at Resaca, between two brigades of Confederates, under General Canty, and the Army of the Tennessee, under Major-General McPherson, who had made a flank movement through Snake Creek Gap, for the purpose of capturing the town and railroad bridge, in Johnston's rear, which lasted till dark, and resulted in the repulse of the Federals.

During the night, General Johnston sent down Hood's corps of three divisions, under Generals Hindman, Cleburne and Walker, and finding these too strong for him, McPherson retreated to Snake Creek Gap and intrenched.

Snake Creek Gap, which played so important a part in this movement, and in shaping the general results of the campaign, cannot be better described than in the following quotation, also, from General Cox:

"Snake Creek is an insignificant branch of the Oostanaula, running southward between high and rugged ridges, which, on the east, are nearly continuous with Rocky Face, and are known by the general name of Chattoogata Mountains. On the west the parallel range is called Horn Mountain. A watershed half way from Tunnel Hill to the Oostanaula separates the sources of Mill Creek from those of Snake Creek, and this divide is properly the gap. The whole pass, however, is known by the name, and is a wild and picturesque defile, five or six miles long. Hardly a cabin was to be seen in its whole length. The road was only such a track as country wagons had worn in the bed of the stream or along the foot of the mountain. The forest shut it in, and only for a little while at midday did the sun enter it. Near its southern extremity * * * it reached the more open country bordering the river, which here runs for a little way nearly west, and roads branch off to Resaca, eastward, and southward to Calhoun, turning the south end of the precipitous ridges, which guard Dalton on the west. Resaca itself stands in the elbow at the junction of the Connasauga with the Oostanaula, and on the north bank of the latter stream. Camp Creek, another small stream, flows into the river just west of the village, and the high plateau bordering it and the more rugged hills between it and the Connasauga a little further north, made it a very strong place for the intrenched camp which the Confederate commander had prepared there."—("ATLANTA," pages 35, 36.)

General Sherman says of this engagement that McPherson:

"* * * had not done the full measure of his work. He had in hand twenty-three thousand of the best men of the army, and could have walked into Resaca (then held only by a small brigade), or he could have placed his whole force astride the railroad above Resaca, and there have easily withstood the attack of Johnston's army, with the knowledge that Thomas and Schofield were on his heels. * * * Such an opportunity does not come twice in a single life; but at the critical moment McPherson seems to have been a little timid. Still he was perfectly justified by his orders, and fell back, and assumed a defensive position in Sugar Valley, on the Resaca side of Snake Creek Gap. As soon as I was informed of this, I determined to pass the whole army through Snake Creek Gap, and move on to Resaca with the main army."—(SHERMAN'S MEMOIRS, Vol. II., pages 34, 35.)

During the next day, another attempt was made upon the Confederates at Mill Creek Gap; but resulted in a Federal repulse.

On the evening of the 11th, General Johnston ordered General Wheeler to move, at daylight the next day, around the end of Rocky Face Ridge, towards Tunnel Hill, with all his available cavalry, to ascertain if the movement southward by the Federal army had been a general one. General Hindman was instructed to support Wheeler with his division. The Confederates encountered Stoneman's cavalry at this point, and drove them back, with a loss to the latter of 150 men and some 400 loaded wagons.

This reconnoissance confirmed the impression that almost the entire Federal army was marching toward Snake Creek Gap, on its way to Resaca.

Accordingly, Dalton * was evacuated the next day by the Confederate army, which retired to Resaca.

" The Federal army approaching Resaca on the Snake Creek Gap road, was met about a mile from the place by Loring's division, and held in check long enough to enable Hardee's and Hood's corps, then just arriving, to occupy their ground undisturbed. As the army was formed (in two lines) Polk's and Hardee's corps were west of the place and railroad, facing to the west; the former on the left, with its left resting on the Oostanaula. Hood's corps extended from Hardee's right across the railroad to the Connasauga, facing to the northwest.

" There was brisk skirmishing all the afternoon of May 13th on Polk's front, and that of Hardee's left division — Cheatham's."—(JOHNSTON'S NARRATIVE, pages 309, 310.)

Early the next day, the skirmishers became engaged along the entire line, beginning on the west. " Those of Polk's corps, from some unaccountable mistake, abandoned their ground, which was regained only by great personal efforts on the part of their field

---

* On August 15, 1864, Dalton was captured by Wheeler's cavalry, who were raiding Sherman's communications. The Confederates secured 200 prisoners and destroyed considerable army stores, etc., and then went northward.

Dalton was also captured by Hood's army on its grand retrograde movement, after the fall of Atlanta. There was a sharp fight south of the town. The Confederates here captured the garrison, a regiment of negro troops. This was on October 13, 1864.

officers.   *   A vigorous assault was made upon Hindman's division; but the assailants were repulsed."

Later on during the day, Lieutenant-General Hood was ordered to attack the Federal left, with Stewart's and Stevenson's divisions. This movement began about six o'clock in the afternoon, and was conducted by the Confederates with admirable precision and vigor, and before dark the Federal left was driven from its ground.

Late in the afternoon, the Federals, under McPherson, however, drove Polk's advanced lines from the hill in front of his left, which commanded the Western & Atlantic Railroad bridge over the Oostanaula.

During the night, the Confederates, under the direction of Colonel Prestman, the chief engineer, made a road, and placed a pontoon bridge across the river, about a mile above

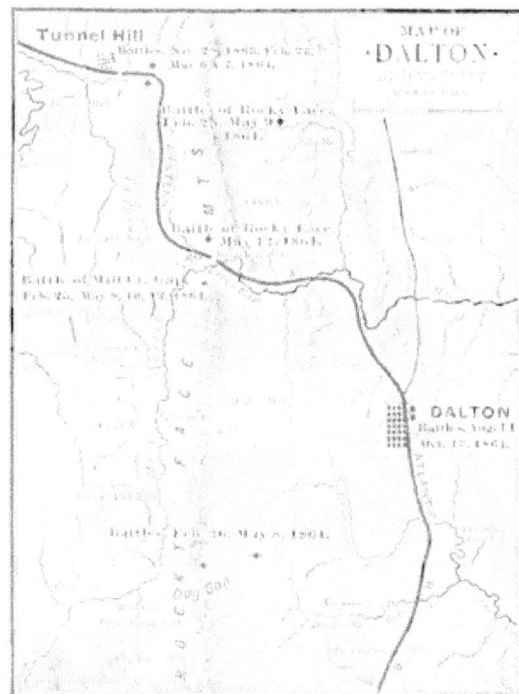

that commanded by the Federal artillery.

On the 15th, sharp skirmishing commenced early, along the whole line, and continued throughout the day. Several determined attacks were made upon Hindman's position; in the last, especially, the assailants exhibited the utmost bravery, many of them reaching the Confederate intrenchments.

The Federals here charged across a broad meadow, from the cover of a wooded ridge, and assaulted the Confederates on the opposite ridge; but, after a bloody struggle, were repulsed. Seeing that they would be subjected to a destructive fire in crossing the valley again, a large portion of them took refuge behind the steep sides of a sort of spur ridge in front of the main one, and there remained until after dark, before venturing back to their former positions.

About noon, a strong force of Federal cavalry captured the hospitals of Hood's corps, which were located east of the Connasauga River. Major-General Wheeler, with Allen's and Hume's brigades, made a gallant attack, and drove off the Federals, however, and pursued them two miles, capturing two standards and some prisoners.

BATTLE OF RINGGOLD, GA
On the line of the Western & Atlantic Railroad
November 27, 1863

GEN. PATRICK R. CLEBURNE,
Commanding Confederate States Forces

GEN. JOSEPH HOOKER,
Commanding United States Forces

During the forenoon, Major-General Stevenson was directed by Lieutenant-General Hood to advance and mask a four-gun battery some eighty yards in front of his line of infantry, which was near the Western & Atlantic Railroad, north of Resaca. Before Stevenson had arranged properly to support it, General Hood ordered him to open its fire. This was done, and a furious attack was immediately made upon it by Hooker's corps, which was facing Hood's at this point. The guns were abandoned by the Confederates, and a very spirited fight for their possession ensued, which resulted in the Federals being driven back from them by the fire of the Confederates; but they found shelter in the neighboring ravine. From this position, their musketry commanded the location of the battery equally as well as did that of the Confederates. A very hot fire was kept up by both sides, which prevented either from removing the guns, and they were consequently left between the two armies until dark, and afterwards seized by the Federals.

These were the only field trophies they captured during the entire campaign to the Chattahoochee River.

At about four P. M. General Stewart, whose division was on the Confederate right, was ordered to attack the Federals, and endeavor to force their line back. General Stevenson was to support him with his division. Hearing of the Lay's Ferry movement, by Sherman, however, General Johnston revoked the order for this assault. The last order did not reach Stewart in time. His troops left their intrenchments and dashed forward in the face of a terrible fire. Not being supported by Stevenson, who had received General Johnston's order, Stewart's men were repulsed with loss.

During the afternoon, General Johnston received notice that the Federals had secured possession of Lay's (or Tanner's) Ferry, nearly three miles west of Calhoun, and were crossing the Oostanaula River in force.

His communications with Atlanta, therefore, being rendered too hazardous, Johnston evacuated Resaca during the night.[*]

The Confederate army, in withdrawing, crossed the river on the railroad bridge and on the pontoon bridge one mile above it. General Stewart's division covered the retreat, remaining in position after the retiring of the other troops on their left had opened to the Federals the way to Resaca and their rear. General Stewart himself was the last man to cross the pontoon bridge, which was then destroyed.

The movement which forced this action on Johnston's part, resulted in a fight at Lay's (or Tanner's) Ferry, on May 14th, whereby the Federal forces secured a crossing, but took no further forward step.

The course of the river, almost parallel to the Western & Atlantic Railroad, protected this advance from Johnston's power of discovery or successful resistance.

On the 15th, Jackson's brigade of Confederates assaulted the Federals, who were encamped east of the Oostanaula, but met a bloody repulse.

---

[*] There was also a vigorous fight at Resaca between the Confederate cavalry and the Federal garrison, October 12, 1864. The Confederates were repulsed. The next day General Hood appeared with his army before the town and demanded its surrender. The demand was refused, and, finding an assault hazardous, Hood moved northward against Dalton.

On the 16th, the Federals, under McPherson, advanced from the ferry, towards Calhoun, driving back the cavalry; but soon came in collision with a portion of Hardee's corps and, in turn, sustained a repulse.

It may be proper here to state that after the war, in disinterring the dead at Resaca, there were found the remains of one hundred and seventy Confederates* and seventeen hundred and ninety Federals. General Sherman, in his dispatch to General Halleck, May 15th, said: "I cannot estimate our dead and wounded up to this hour; but it will not fall much short of three thousand (3,000)."

Johnston fell back to Adairsville; but, finding that the breadth of the Oothcaloga Valley exceeded so much the front of his army, properly formed for battle, that he could obtain no advantage of ground, ordered the troops to move to Cassville.

During the afternoon of the 17th, the Federals struck the Confederate rear-guard at Adairsville; but, after a sharp conflict with Wheeler's cavalry and Cheatham's division of infantry, were checked. During the night the Confederates evacuated this position.

Johnston, correctly supposing that the Federal army, in pressing the pursuit, would divide, so as to secure passage over more than one road, ordered a vigilant watch kept, with the intention of endeavoring to crush one wing before the other could come to its relief. The Federal movement being as he foresaw, he ordered Polk to engage, in front, the column coming down the road by the railroad, and Hood to attack it in flank when Polk's firing began in front. Hood, however, acting on erroneous information about the Federal movement, made a different disposition of his line. So much time was lost in correcting this mistake, that the intended attack was given over, as its success depended upon its being properly timed.

Of this movement, General Sherman says:

"Thomas's head of column which had followed the country roads alongside of the railroad, was about four miles east of Kingston, towards Cassville, when, about noon I got a message from him that he had found the enemy, drawn up in line of battle, on some extensive, open ground about half way between Kingston and Cassville, and that appearances indicated a willingness and preparation for battle.

"Hurriedly sending orders to McPherson to resume the march, to hasten forward by roads leading to the south of Kingston, so as to leave for Thomas's troops and trains the use of the main road, and to come up on his right, I rode forward rapidly over some rough gravel hills, and about six miles from Kingston found General Thomas, with his troops deployed; but he reported that the enemy had fallen back in echelon of divisions, steadily and in superb order, into Cassville."— (MEMOIRS, Vol. II., pages 37, 38.)

On the 19th of May, Johnston took position near Cassville for what he intended should be the great battle of the campaign.

Of this he says:

"The Confederate army was drawn up in a position that I remember as the best that I saw occupied during the war — the ridge immediately south of Cassville with a broad, open, elevated valley in front of it, completely commanded by the fire of troops occupying its crest. The

---

* There is now a Confederate cemetery just above Resaca. Several hundred Southern soldiers here "sleep the sleep that knows no waking."

eastern end of this ridge is perhaps a mile to the east of Cassville. Its southwest end is near the railroad, a little to the west of Cass Station. Its length was just sufficient for Hood's and Polk's corps, and half of Hardee's, formed, as usual, in two lines, and in that order from right to left. The other half of Hardee's troops prolonging the line, were southwest of the railroad on undulating ground, on which they had only such advantage as their own labor, directed by engineering, could give them. They worked with great spirit, however, and were evidently full of confidence. This gave me assurance of success on the right and in the center, where we had very decided advantage of ground." (JOHNSTON'S NARRATIVE, page 322.)

During the afternoon, the Federal artillery commenced firing upon Hood's and Polk's troops. This, with a heavy skirmish fire, continued until dusk.

CAPTURE OF A FEDERAL WAGON TRAIN.
Near Cassville, Ga., May 21, 1864.

The beautiful village of Cassville was between the two lines. The contest about the village was very severe, especially between the batteries, which were posted on the ridges confronting each other. Sharp skirmishing and fighting occurred on the streets. Many of the houses were riddled with balls, and the fine college buildings, especially, were pierced through with shot and shell. Some of the dwellings were also fired by these and consumed.

At a council of war, held that night, Generals Hood and Polk expressed to General Johnston their fears that they could not hold the positions assigned them, because of a possible enfilading fire from a Federal battery on the opposite ridge. General Hardee stated that he could hold his position, although it was a less favorable one, so far as the nature of the ground was concerned.

Johnston was very unwilling to abandon the position without a battle; but finally, in deference to the judgment of two of his three Lieutenant-Generals, consented to do so; and accordingly fell back to the Etowah River, and crossed it the next day.

On the 22d of the month, General Wheeler was instructed to go north of the river with his cavalry, and ascertain the movements of the Federal army. He soon received information that Sherman was moving westward, as if to cross the Etowah near Stilesboro and Euharlee, and on the 24th, in the vicinity of Cassville, encountered the troops guarding a large supply train. A sharp fight ensued between Wheeler's cavalry and the Federals, which resulted in the capture of 182 prisoners, about 200 wagons, with army stores, etc. The Confederates brought across the Etowah River 70 of these loaded wagons, with their teams, contents, etc., and burned the rest.

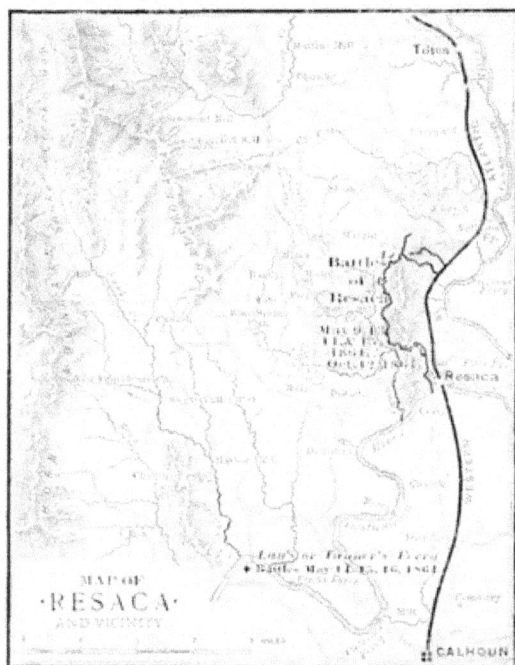

MAP OF
·RESACA·
AND VICINITY

The information secured by Wheeler showed that Sherman had evidently determined not to move directly against the very strong position at Allatoona Pass, on the Western & Atlantic Railroad; but to proceed, via Dallas and Burnt Hickory, against Marietta. This movement was a difficult one, being through a rough, densely-wooded country, with few roads and these very indifferent, and, furthermore, away from the railroad, his main channel for supplies.

On the 23d, therefore, Lieutenant-General Hardee was ordered, by General Johnston, to march, by New Hope Church, to the road leading from Stilesboro through Dallas to Atlanta, and Lieutenant-General Polk to move to the same road, by a route further to the left. Lieutenant-General Hood was directed to follow Hardee the next day. Hardee's corps reached the point designated to them, that afternoon. Polk's was then within four or five miles of it, to the east, and Hood's within four miles of New Hope Church, on the road to it from Allatoona. On the 25th he reached New Hope Church early in the day. Learning that the Federal army was in close proximity, its right at Dallas, and its line extending towards Allatoona, General Hood was ordered by General Johnston to form his corps parallel to the road by which he had marched, with his centre opposite the church. General Polk was instructed to place his in line with it, but about five miles from this position, on the left; and General Hardee was ordered to occupy the ridge extending from General Polk's corps across the road leading from Dallas toward Atlanta, his left division, Bate's, holding that road.

During the afternoon, Hood's advanced lines, consisting of one regiment, encountered Hooker's corps. A gallant fight ensued; but the Confederates were driven back to Stewart's division. Late in the afternoon, heavy cannonading was opened upon Hood's center division, Stewart's, opposite New Hope Church. This was soon supplemented by an attack in line of battle by Hooker's corps, in such deep order that it presented a front equal only to that of Stewart's first line, of three brigades. The firing at once became general, and the Federal advance was very steady and resolute, until within some fifty paces of the Confederate lines. Here, however, they paused, and then fell back. They again advanced, and pushed as near the Confederate line as before; but so desperate was the resistance, and so hot the fire of musketry and artillery, that the assailants were again compelled to retire.

While the combat was raging, a shell from one of the Federal batteries burst between Generals Johnston and Hood, who were standing but a few yards apart, near the church; but fortunately neither of them was hurt.

In this action portions of two Confederate brigades were partially sheltered by some fallen timber, which, finding near their line, they had hastily thrown into position. The other brigade had no protection.

The night, which came on, was very dark, with heavy rains; and there was much confusion in both armies, as they were endeavoring to assume position, facing each other, among the thickly-wooded hills, and each industriously working, though in the darkness, to strengthen its ground against any sudden assault by its enemy.

General Sherman says:

"I slept on the ground without cover, alongside of a log, got little sleep, resolved at daylight to renew the battle, and to make a lodgment on the Dallas and Allatoona road if possible, but the morning revealed a strong line of intrenchments facing us, with a heavy force of infantry and guns. The battle was renewed and without success."—(Memoirs, Vol. II., page 44.)

That morning, the Confederates found the Federal line extending much further east than it was the day before.

In the afternoon, quite a sharp fight occurred between a large body of Federal cavalry and Avery's regiment of Georgia cavalry. Although desperately wounded, Colonel Avery continued to command, and maintained the contest until the arrival of re-enforcements, who held the position.

The Federals kept rapidly extending their line to their left, the Confederates being forced thereby to counter movements, which soon brought on another engagement.

Late in the afternoon of the 27th, a bloody struggle ensued between Cleburne's division of Hardee's corps, aided by a portion of Wheeler's dismounted cavalry, and the Fourth Army corps of Federals, under command of General Howard, in columns six lines deep, near Pickett's Mill and the road leading from Burnt Hickory.

The latter assailed the Confederates with great courage, and pressed forward with fortitude under fire, which will ever be remembered with admiration by those who met them. The two lines were at one time within twenty paces of each other; but, at length, the Federals were compelled to give way before the terrific storm of bullets; and fled for refuge to a ravine near by.

About ten o'clock that night, ascertaining that many of the Federal troops were in the ravine before them, the Confederates charged and drove them out, taking some 232 prisoners.

The scene of the struggle was in a dense wood, with thick undergrowth, broken by hills and ravines, where nothing could be observed at a distance, and where neither side could see what was going on, except at the immediate point of conflict.

The acknowledged loss of the Federals in this combat was about 1,500 men. Cleburne's loss was 85 killed and 363 wounded.

Among other trophies, the Confederates captured some 1,200 small arms.

General Johnston records the following touching incident of this fight:

"When the United States troops paused in their advance, within fifteen paces of the Texan front rank, one of their color-bearers planted his colors eight or ten feet in front of his regiment, and was instantly shot dead; a soldier sprang forward to his place, and fell also, as he grasped the color-staff; a second and third followed successively, and each received death as speedily as his predecessors; a fourth, however, seized and bore back the object of soldierly devotion."— (NARRATIVE, pages 330, 331.)

On the morning of the 28th, the Confederates, having formed the idea that the greater portion of the Federal army had been withdrawn towards the position in front of the Confederate right, determined to seize the works opposite their left, and thus turn Sherman's right; but, after meeting hot resistance from artillery and infantry, were repulsed with a loss of several hundred men.

This assault (by Bate's division of Hardee's corps) was made upon Logan's corps, consisting of Harrow's, Smith's and Osterhaus's divisions. Three guns of the First Iowa battery, which had been run out near the skirmish line, were captured by the Confeder-

ates: but they could not take them off. The assaulting columns were caught by both a front and a cross fire from the breastworks. The Federal General Cox says that "the enemy" charged up to the intrenchments "with the most determined courage, and, though suffering terribly, was not driven back till he had inflicted considerable loss upon us, some of our bravest and best officers being among the killed and wounded." He further says:

"The night following (May 29th) another effort was made against McPherson, and the alarm ran down the whole line. Nearly all of Johnston's batteries opened from right to left, and skirmish lines were pushed up close to Sherman's works. The night was dark, and along the centre, where the valley was open, the flashing artillery from the hilltops, and the flying and bursting shells made a magnificent spectacle, but it ended in display. It drew fire enough from McPherson to prove that he was still there, and this was probably all that the enemy intended by it."

Of the general operations during this period, the two great commanders bear witness as follows:

"The Federal intrenched line was extended daily toward the railroad in the direction of Allatoona. We endeavored to keep pace with this extension, to prevent being cut off from the railroad and Marietta. But, from the great inequality of force, two or three miles of the right of ours was occupied by dismounted cavalry in skirmishing order. The enemy's demonstrations against this part of our front led to skirmishing with Wheeler's troops, in which the latter captured above a hundred prisoners between the 1st and 4th of June. The infantry skirmishers of the two armies were incessantly engaged at the same time, from right to left, when there was light enough to distinguish and aim at a man."—(JOHNSTON'S NARRATIVE, page 335.)

"Meantime Thomas and Schofield were completing their deployments, gradually overlapping Johnston on his right, and thus extending our left nearer and nearer to the railroad, the nearest point of which was Acworth, about eight miles distant. All this time a continual battle was in progress by strong skirmish lines, taking advantage of every species of cover, and both parties fortifying each night by rifle-trenches, with head-logs, many of which grew to be as formidable as first-class works of defence. Occasionally one party or the other would make a dash in the nature of a sally, but usually it sustained a repulse with great loss of life. I visited personally all parts of our lines, nearly every day, was constantly within musket range, and though the fire of musketry and cannon resounded day and night along the whole line, varying from six to ten miles, I rarely saw a dozen of the enemy at any one time, and these were always skirmishers dodging from tree to tree, or behind logs on the ground, or who occasionally showed their heads above the hastily constructed but remarkably strong rifle-pits."—(SHERMAN'S MEMOIRS, Vol. II., page 45.)

On the 4th of June, the Federal army being concentrated principally on its left, near the railroad, and covered by its long line of intrenchments, the Confederates abandoned Allatoona and Acworth, and fell back to a new position, near Kennesaw Mountain, its left wing resting on Lost Mountain, and its right extending east of the Western & Atlantic Railroad and behind Noonday Creek.

Of this change of base, General Sherman says:

"On the 1st of June, General McPherson closed in upon the right, and, without attempting further to carry the enemy's strong position at New Hope Church, I held our general right in close contact with it, gradually, carefully, and steadily working by the left, until our strong infantry lines had reached and secured possession of all the wagon roads between New Hope, Allatoona and Acworth, when I dispatched Generals Garrard's and Stoneman's divisions of cavalry into Allatoona, the first around by the west end of the pass, and the latter by the direct road. Both reached their destination without opposition, and orders were at once given to repair the railroad forward from Kingston to Allatoona, embracing the bridge across the Etowah River.

"Thus the real object of my move on Dallas was accomplished, and on the 4th of June I was preparing to draw off from New Hope Church, and to take position on the railroad in front of Allatoona, when General Johnston himself having evacuated his position, we effected the change without further battle, and moved to the railroad, occupying it from Allatoona and Acworth forward to Big Shanty, in sight of the famous Kennesaw Mountain.   *   *   *   *

"With the drawn battle of New Hope Church, and our occupation of the natural fortress of Allatoona, terminated the month of May, and the first stage of the campaign."—(SHERMAN'S MEMOIRS, Vol. II., pages 46, 49.)

Thus fell Allatoona, which General Sherman calls "the gate through the last, or most eastern (western?) spur of the Alleghanies." He fortified it strongly, with a fort on each side of the pass through which the Western & Atlantic Railroad runs, about 120 feet below, and made it his secondary base of supplies, with Acworth as the place of issue.

Johnston could justly console himself with the knowledge that the position was wrested from him not by assault, nor so much by pure strategy as by "two to one;" but, with the coveted prize in his grasp, Sherman could well afford to feel independent of the criticism which minified the glory of the achievement.

Just here is probably the best place to interject a short reference to a subsequent occurrence which has linked the name of Allatoona with one of the most stirring gospel lyrics of the English tongue.

After the fall of Atlanta, when Hood was making his famous movement toward and into Tennessee, in Sherman's rear, he sent General French, with his division, to seize Allatoona, where General Sherman had stored over a million rations of bread.

Learning of this movement, General Sherman signaled from MacRae's Hill, at Vining's Station, on the Western & Atlantic Railroad, to the signal station on the crest of Kennesaw Mountain, and thence in turn the message was transmitted over the heads of the Confederates, "through the sky," to the forts on Allatoona heights, for General John M. Corse, at Rome, Ga., to be notified that he must at once hasten to Allatoona with re-inforcements for the garrison at that important point.

Corse, with the least possible delay, started from Rome at eight P. M., October 4, 1864, and arrived at Allatoona at one A. M., October 5th. He brought 1,054 men to re-inforce Colonel Tourtellotte's garrison of 890, thus making a total, for the defence, of 1,944.

He found the outposts already engaged, and, as soon as daylight came, he drew back the men from the village to the ridge on which the two forts were built.

These, by the way, were connected by a bridge which spanned the deep railroad cut.

Soon thereafter a lively bombardment was opened from a Confederate battery on a high hill a few hundred yards to the south; and, at about eight A. M., the assault began, coming from front, flank and rear.

General Sherman says:

"These redoubts had been located * * * at the time of our advance on Kennesaw, the previous June. Each redoubt overlooked the storehouses close by the railroad, and each could aid the other defensively by catching in flank the attacking force of the other. Our troops at first endeavored to hold some ground outside the redoubts, but were soon driven inside, when the enemy made repeated assaults, but were always driven back. About eleven A. M., Colonel Redfield, of the Thirty-ninth Iowa, was killed, and Colonel Rowett was wounded, but never ceased to fight and encourage his men. Colonel Tourtellotte was shot through the hips, but continued to command. General Corse was at one P. M., shot across the face, the ball cutting his ear, which stunned him, but he continued to encourage his men and to give orders. The enemy (about half past one P. M.) made a last and desperate effort to carry one of the redoubts, but was badly cut to pieces by the artillery and infantry fire from the other, when he began to draw off, leaving his dead and wounded on the ground."—(Memoirs, Vol. II., page 149.)

General French's assaulting force in this battle was about 2,000 men. The Federal loss, officially reported, was 707 men. General French's official report shows that his total loss was 799 men. He also states that the attack failed because his ammunition gave out, as Hood was not aware that Allatoona was fortified, and ordered him there to fill up the railroad cut. The above figures, however, show how desperate were both the attack and the defense. The deep cut through which the railroad runs was strown with dead and wounded men on that fatal day.

The Confederate retreat was hastened by the information received during the battle, that General Cox's division was rapidly approaching from Kennesaw Mountain, to the relief of the garrison, and was close at hand.*

Early in the day, General Sherman, who was on the top of Kennesaw Mountain, succeeded in exchanging messages with the signal station on Allatoona heights. He received intelligence that Corse had arrived; and signaled back, "Hold the fort; for I am coming."

From this message, and the attendant thrilling circumstances, have come the gospel hymn, which is now sung wherever the English language is being used for evangelizing the world:

> "Ho! my comrades, see the signal
> Waving in the sky!
> Re-enforcements now appearing,
> Victory is nigh!
> Chorus.—"Hold the fort; for I am coming," etc.

The most characteristic memorial of this bloody and famous struggle, which now salutes the eye of the tourist, as the train darts through the deep, fern-lined pass, is a lone grave at its northwestern end, immediately by the track, on the west side. This is the resting place of a Confederate soldier, who was buried on the spot where he fell.

For years past the track-hands of the Western & Atlantic Railroad have held this grave under their special charge, and made attention to it a sacred duty. Whenever their

---

* On their retreat, the Confederates came to the block-house, which the Federals had built at the railroad bridge over Allatoona Creek. General French summoned the garrison to surrender. They refused, and he then opened a hot musketry fire upon them, and also turned his cannon against the position. These soon forced the raising of the white flag.

BATTLE OF ALLATOONA, GA.
At Allatoona Pass, on the Western & Atlantic Railroad.
October 6, 1864.

Gen. S. G. French,
Commanding Confederate States Forces.

Gen. Jno. M. Corse,
Commanding United States Forces.

periodic rounds bring them hither, they see that it is kept clear of rubbish, and that the head- and foot-stones are firm.

A neat marble head-stone has been placed here, on which is the following inscription:

An
UNKNOWN HERO.
He died for the cause
he thought was right.

The *Marietta Journal* thus touchingly refers to this memorial:

THE SOLDIER'S GRAVE.
On the Western & Atlantic Railroad, in Allatoona Pass.

"He was some mother's darling, and perhaps when the cruel war was over, she wiped her tear-bedimmed eyes and through her spectacles watched for the coming of her soldier boy, but he came not. Still she prayed and gazed down the road and scanned the face of every passer-by; every foot step that sounded on the walk her eager ears caught up with expectancy; her heart beat faster and thrilled with hope; her eyes kindled with joy; her wrinkled face lighted up with a smile, and her old arms, no doubt, involuntarily went out to clasp to her bosom her darling boy; but she was doomed to disappointment; it was her neighbor's boy who had returned, and not her's; and sadly she turned back to her old arm chair by the window, she choked down the heart sobs and cleared away the unbidden tears, and wondered why *her* boy did not come. No tidings came of his whereabouts. She did not know that the boy whom she saw proudly leave home in his new suit of gray in response to his country's call, at that moment filled an unknown grave. Perhaps, after many years of waiting, she too has gone over the river of death, and, with her boy, will be a shadowy witness of the erection of the head-stone to the memory of 'An Unknown Hero.'"

Taking up again the thread of our narrative, General Sherman says of the new position assumed by the Confederate army, after falling back from New Hope Church and Allatoona:

"On the 10th day of June, the whole combined army moved forward six miles to Big Shanty, a station on the railroad; whence we had a good view of the enemy's position, which embraced three prominent hills, known as Kennesaw, Pine Mountain and Lost Mountain. On each of these hills the enemy had signal stations and fresh lines of parapets. Heavy masses of infantry could be distinctly seen with the naked eye, and it was manifest that Johnston had chosen his ground well, and with deliberation had prepared for battle; but his line was at least ten miles in extent, too long in my judgment to be held successfully by his force, then estimated at sixty thousand. As his position, however, gave him a perfect view over our field, we had to proceed with due caution. McPherson had the left, following the railroad, which curved around the north base of Kennesaw; Thomas, the center, obliqued to the right, deployed below Kennesaw and facing Pine Hill; and Schofield, somewhat refused, was on the general right; looking south, toward Lost Mountain."—(MEMOIRS, Vol. II., page 51.)

Early in June, there was quite a sharp cavalry fight near Big Shanty, in which the Confederates were successful.

During the next few days, the cavalry on both sides was very active; there being almost constant skirmishing in the neighborhood of the railroad. This had been torn up by the Confederates, but was rebuilt by the Federals, and, on the 12th, the Etowah bridge having been restored, the Confederates heard the whistle of the locomotives arriving at Big Shanty.*

The lines of the two armies were constantly being drawn closer to each other, and, by the 14th of June, it became evident that those of the Confederates were too attenuated for them to longer hold Pine Mountain.

Generals Johnston, Hardee and Polk, accordingly, rode to the top of this mountain, which was held by Bate's division, to view the situation, and select some better position. Their presence attracted a body of soldiers; and General Sherman, seeing the group, and supposing that it might possibly be well to scatter them, told General Howard to order the commander of one of his batteries to fire upon them. General Polk was struck in the breast by an unexploded shell and killed. His death filled the entire South with grief.

The next morning there was a general advance by the Federal army against the Confederate positions, in which Blair's freshly-arrived corps of McPherson's army carried a spur of the hills, near the railroad, commanding the intrenched line of Hood's skirmishers, and forced Hood back behind Noonday Creek. By this movement an entire Alabama regiment was surrounded and captured.

The same morning, Thomas pushed his front sharply to the east of Pine Mountain. The Confederate advanced-guard held the trenches connecting their principal lines with the mountain, and also some other detached works covering these. Hooker, with his corps, assaulted these works, and, after quite a struggle, captured them. He then hurled Geary's division against the main line; but here met, in Cleburne, more than his match, and, after a very gallant fight, Geary was forced to give over the attempt, with a loss of several hundred men.

On the 15th of June, the Confederates abandoned Pine Mountain; and, on the 16th, the Federals, having secured possession of some high ground from which their artillery

---

* Big Shanty is famous as being the place where occurred the "Capture of a Locomotive," April 12, 1862. Here, about twenty Federal soldiers, in disguise, seized an engine and three cars, and dashed northward, with the intention of burning the bridges on the Western & Atlantic Railroad. After a hot pursuit they were overtaken and captured near Ringgold. The "General," the engine they seized, is still pulling a passenger train on the W. & A. R. R.

was able to enfilade a good portion of Hardee's line, and also to sweep the road from Gilgal Church to Marietta, for some distance, it was found necessary to evacuate Lost Mountain also.

They accordingly fell back to a position on the high grounds east of Mud Creek, about one mile west of the western end of Kennesaw Mountain, facing to the west. Their extreme left occupied the crest of a steep cliff, on which General Hardee had planted some batteries which commanded the deep, wide valley in their front, across the creek.

Finding, however, that a portion of their line was exposed to an enfilading fire from the Federal batteries on the opposite hills, and, the Federal right having been extended till it turned Hardee's flank, the Confederates, after obstinate fighting during the 18th, in

THE RIFLE-PITS BEFORE KENNESAW.
June, 1864.

which Wood's and Newton's divisions of Howard's corps captured and held a portion of their outer works, retired to another position, which included the crest of Kennesaw Mountain, thence running to its western end, and, from this, southward some three miles.

General Johnston says of this movement:

"Another position, including the crest of Kennesaw, was chosen on the 17th, and prepared for occupation under the direction of Colonel Prestman. The troops were placed on this line on the

19th: Hood's corps massed between the railroad and that from Marietta to Canton; Loring's, with a division (his own, commanded by Featherston) between the railroad and eastern base of the mountain; and Walthall's and French's along the crest of the short ridge. French's left reaching its southwestern base, and Hardee's from French's left almost due south across the Lost Mountain and Marietta Road, to the brow of the high ground immediately north of the branch of Nose's Creek that runs from Marietta. Walker's division on the right, Bate's next, then Cleburne's and Cheatham's on the left."—(JOHNSTON'S NARRATIVE, pages 338, 339.)

The Federal General Cox also says:

"The key of the new Confederate line was Kennesaw Mountain, which is the summit of the watershed, and whose wood-covered sides, breaking down into deep ravines, made an impregnable military position, whilst its summit, overlooking the country in all directions, made concealment of movements on Sherman's part next to impossible."—("ATLANTA," page 103.)

During this period, there had been for over three weeks almost daily rains, which raised the streams, and, by making the roads nearly impassable, were a source of great annoyance to both armies. On more than one occasion, full-line attacks had been made in the midst of furious thunderstorms, which, it is said, "made it difficult to distinguish between the discharges of artillery, at close quarters, and the rattling thunder."

During this same period, also, there was daily skirmishing between the two armies from one end of the line to the other, and, while the sun shone, there was scarcely an hour in which one could not hear the incessant "pop," "pop" of musketry, from the riflepits, which dotted the hillsides and woody valleys, or from behind the trees, fences, or any species of cover which the combatants could secure. This frequently lasted until far into the night, when the continuous flashes of light in the forest simulated the appearance of myriads of fire-flies. The losses by both armies, from this species of warfare, were heavier than in the main engagements.

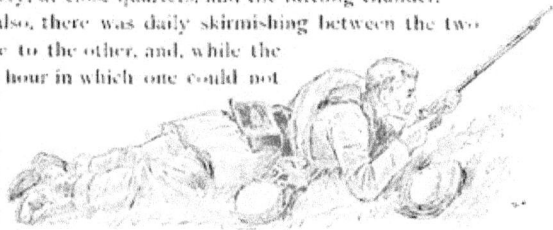

On the 20th, the most considerable cavalry fight of the campaign occurred, on the Confederate right, between the commands of Wheeler and Garrard. The Federals were worsted in this affair, and lost two standards, etc.

The Federal army, during this same period, was making constant extensions southward, which forced corresponding movements by the Confederates.

Hood's corps was transferred from the Confederate right to their extreme left; and Johnston ordered Hood to endeavor to prevent any progress of Sherman's right toward the railroad, the latter and the Confederate intrenchments being nearly parallel, and scarcely more than three miles apart. General Johnston says, "Our position, consequently, was a very hazardous one."

During this same period the Confederates were placing batteries upon the twin crests of Kennesaw Mountain. Big Kennesaw, the higher of the two, runs up into a peak about six or seven hundred feet above the surrounding country, affording room for only a few guns. Little Kennesaw, on the contrary, consists of a commanding ridge, extending for from seven hundred to a thousand feet, before the descent begins at each end; and is a magnificent position for artillery. General French, whose division covered this ridge, on about the 20th of the month, planted twenty guns upon it. The road leading to the crest being difficult of ascent, and exposed to the fire of the Federal batteries on the neighboring heights, the Confederates, after some search, found a route behind the mountain, up which they dragged the guns by ropes (prolongues). This labor was undertaken late in the evening, and continued through the night, and, by daylight next morning, Guibo's and Ward's batteries were planted on Little Kennesaw, behind strongly constructed works. Hoskins's battery was also placed on the descending slope of the western end of the ridge, to command the approaches to the infantry line farther down. The timber growth on the mountain concealed these from the view of the Federals.

On the morning of the 22d, a furious bombardment was opened, from these batteries, upon the Federal camps and intrenchments, in the fields and forests below, which compelled a disorderly retreat to the rear by the wagon trains, etc., and greatly annoyed the forces manning the breastworks. Towards night the Confederates opened these guns again upon their enemy; and at eleven P. M. the bombardment was renewed. In the darkness this is said to have presented a magnificent spectacle to those on the surrounding hills and valleys, the flashes of light, and the glare on the rising clouds of smoke, seeming to crown the lordly mountain with a tiara of fire.

Within the next day or so, General Sherman, it is stated, brought 120 guns to bear against this position, which number was increased later to 140. From these the bombardment of the batteries on the crest of the mountain is said to have been terrific, and to have virtually silenced the Confederate guns. The top of the ridge was covered with trees and limbs felled by the shells. Thousands of these passed high over the mountain, exploding in the air; or, falling in the forest, spread destruction almost amid the very suburbs of Marietta.

On the 22d of June, occurred quite a hot fight between Hood's corps, and Schofield's and Hooker's troops. The Federals attacked the Confederates, but were repulsed. The latter, in turn, attempted to carry the Federal position; but, after seizing a line of breastworks, suffered a severe repulse.

In an assault upon an intrenched battery, on a high, bare hill, they were driven back, after a bloody fight, with a loss of about 1,000 men. This is usually known as the battle of Kulp's (or, more properly, Kolb's,) Farm.

The general situation at about this period is well summarized in a dispatch from General Sherman to General Halleck, dated June 23d:

"We continue to press forward on the principle of an advance against fortified positions. The whole country is one vast fort, and Johnston must have at least fifty miles of connected trenches with abatis and finished batteries. We gain ground daily, fighting all the time. * * * Our lines are now in close contact, and the fighting is incessant, with a good deal of artillery fire. As fast as we gain one position the enemy has another all ready, but I think he will soon have to let go Kennesaw, which is the key to the whole country. The weather is now better, and the roads are drying up fast."— (Memoirs, Vol. II., pages 59, 60.)

It is not improper to state here that the country around Kennesaw Mountain, New Hope Church and Allatoona, is broken up into numerous detached hills and irregular ridges; divided by ravines or narrow valleys. It was impossible, therefore, for an army, largely outnumbered, to procure any line of defence, several miles long, which would be, at all points, strong, inasmuch as its enemy, apart from the power to turn its flanks, could also find numerous high places in its immediate front overlooking and commanding its positions across the occasional valleys; while the thick cover of the forests and undergrowth veiled the movements of troops, being massed for a rush upon its weak points, or for the attack upon steep hills, whose armed occupants were, by the nature of the ground, even sometimes in the middle of the line, isolated from necessary support.

While in nowise detracting, therefore, from the bravery and fortitude of the Federal soldiery, which certainly won its laurels in this momentous and picturesque campaign, yet the masterly skill and strategic genius displayed by Johnston in handling his army, which was faced and flanked in this craggy wilderness by a force which had two muskets to its one, and the cheerful endurance and persistent courage of his men, and their enthusiastic devotion to and confidence in their commander, were almost wonderful.

On the 24th of June, a very vigorous attack was made upon Hardee's position, immediately southwest of Kennesaw Mountain. On the next day a portion of Hood's corps, on the Confederate left, was likewise assaulted; but, in each instance, the Federals were repulsed.

These daily combats, and extensions of the Federal lines, also, made those of the Confederates so long, and so harrassed them, that there was serious danger of the Federals breaking through at some weak point. Sherman, with his preponderance of numbers, was evidently aiming to accomplish this very result, if possible. In fact, he says:

"During the 24th and 25th of June General Schofield extended his right as far as prudent, so as to compel the enemy to thin out his lines correspondingly, with the intention to make two strong assaults at points where success would give us the greatest advantage. * * * I reasoned that if we could make a breach anywhere near the rebel centre, and thrust in a strong head of column, that with the one moiety of our army we could hold in check the corresponding wing of the enemy, and with the other sweep in flank and overwhelm the other half."—(Memoirs, Vol. II., page 60.)

At about ten o'clock in the morning of the 25th, the Confederate batteries on the crest of Kennesaw opened fire upon the Federals. The latter replied furiously, and for an hour there was a grand artillery duel. This was renewed during the afternoon, and was a majestic spectacle; but the damage to both sides was small.

General French thus graphically describes the situation on this date:

"From the top of the mountain the vast panorama is ever changing. There are now large trains to the left of Lost Mountain and at Big Shanty, and wagons are moving to and fro everywhere. Encampments of hospitals, quartermasters, commissaries, cavalry, and infantry whiten the plain here and there as far as the eye can reach. Our side of the line looks narrow, poor, and lifeless, with but little canvass in spots that contrasts with the green foliage.

"The usual flank extension is going on. Troops on both sides move to left, and now the blue smoke of the musket discloses the line by day trending away, far away south toward the Chattahoochee, and by night it is marked, at times, by the red glow of the artillery, amidst the spark-like flash of small arms that looks in the distance like innumerable fire-flies."

After these preliminary contests, which severely tested the bravery and endurance of both armies, on the 27th of June, 1864, occurred the great and famous battle of Kennesaw Mountain; which was probably the distinctive battle between Dalton and Atlanta, of the Atlanta campaign — a battle which will ever hold its position, on the page of history, as being one which conferred imperishable lustre upon the valor of American soldiery — the attack being made with vigor, pluck and persistence, which in themselves eminently deserved success, and being met with such courage and fortitude as alone could have made the efforts of their antagonists futile.

Of this memorable struggle, the two commanding Generals summarize as follows:

"In the morning of the 27th, after a furious cannonade, the Federal army made a general assault upon the Confederate position, — which was received everywhere with firmness, and repelled with a loss to the assailants enormously disproportionate to that which they inflicted. At several points the characteristic fortitude of the Northwestern soldiers held them under a close and destructive fire long after reasonable hope of success was gone. The attack upon Loring's corps was by the Army of Tennessee; that upon Hardee's by the Army of the Cumberland. The principal efforts of the enemy were directed against Loring's right and left brigades, and the left of Hardee's corps." — (Johnston's Narrative, page 341.)

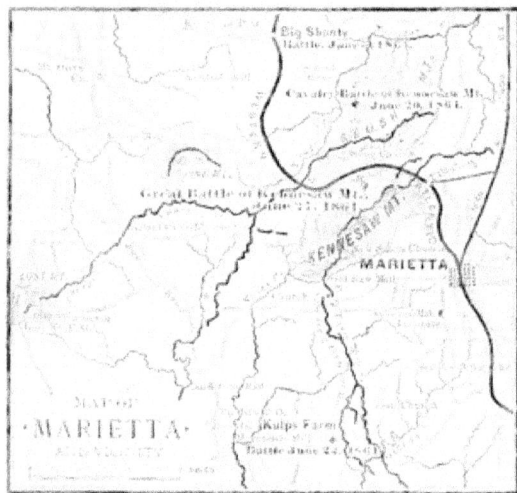

"About 9 A. M. of the day appointed the troops moved to the assault, and all along our lines for ten miles a furious fire of artillery and musketry was kept up. At all points the enemy met us with determined courage and in great force. McPherson's attacking column fought up the face of the lesser Kennesaw, but could not reach the summit. About a mile to the right (just below the Dallas Road) Thomas's assaulting column reached the parapet, where Brigadier-General Harker was shot down, mortally wounded, and Brigadier-General McCook (my old law partner) was desperately wounded, from the effects of which he afterwards died. By 11.30 the assault was in fact over, and had failed. We had not broken the rebel line at either point, but our assaulting columns held their ground within a few yards of the rebel trenches, and there covered themselves with parapet." — (Sherman's Memoirs, Vol. II., pages 60, 61.)

It would be hard to attempt to go into details of this masterly combat without being betrayed into a requisition for very much more space than this little publication will admit.

The attempt upon the Confederate right, which lay east of Kennesaw Mountain, running across the Western & Atlantic Railroad, and north of the present station,

Joseph E. Brown

Elizabeth, to the hills, some hundreds of yards beyond, was by Logan's corps, formed in three lines, and supported by Blair and Dodge, with their respective corps, a portion of which fronted the mountain also, and made strong demonstrations against it, accompanying them with heavy and constant firing. They first fell upon Nelson's (Twelfth Louisiana) regiment, which occupied a strong line of rifle-pits, six hundred yards in front of the main intrenchments. These held their ground, keeping up a hot fusilade, until the first Federal ranks had approached within twenty-five paces, and then hastily retired to the Confederate line of battle.

The Federal troops advanced steadily, and soon came within musket shot of Featherston's entire front. A destructive fire was here opened upon them from the intrenchments, which compelled a halt; but, taking position in the forest, amid the tangled undergrowth, they kept, in return, a furious fire upon the Confederates. The batteries upon the mountain, and those located along Featherston's lines, poured forth a terrific storm of shot and shell upon their front and flanks. For almost an hour they gamely held their position, unable to advance and reluctant to retreat; but, at length, having lost seven commanding officers of regiments and hundreds of men, some of them within thirty feet of the Confederates' principal works, Logan ordered his men to retire to the line of rifle-pits they had first captured.

During this same time an impetuous assault was made upon Wheeler's troops, and Quarles's brigade of Walthall's division, in front of and upon the mountain, in the shelter of rifle-pits. A body of Federals charged into Quarles's rifle-pits, where most of them were killed or captured. Many of the Federals, also, were picked off by the Confederate skirmishers, firing from behind trees, rocks, etc., on the side of the mountain. These were scattered irregularly among the crags and forest growth below the Confederate breast-works; but high enough above the field to command a full view over it, and the Federal advance, which is said to have been made by a portion of Blair's corps.

Against the lesser Kennesaw there was a heavy demonstration and hot fire maintained in front; and a very vigorous charge was made upon the western end of the mountain, which was held by French's division.

The attack upon Cockrell's Missouri brigade, which occupied the extreme west of the ridge, on French's left, was very determined and impetuous—the Federal advance driving in the skirmishers, and pressing resolutely forward till within about twenty paces of the Confederate line; but here it was met by a cool steadiness which checked and finally repulsed it. This attempt was principally by Howard's corps, under the cover of the concentration of about fifty field-pieces, which, bursting forth from battery to battery, were bombarding the Confederate position with terrible fury. The assailing columns likewise advanced rapidly from the west, and dashed fiercely through the skirmishers on Walker's right, immediately south of the mountain, taking in reverse those on the right and left, while they were also being attacked in front. Within a few minutes about eighty of Walker's men, it is said, had been bayoneted or captured in their rifle-pits.

Walker's line was assaulted with great vigor; but here, in addition to the musketry fire from his front, the Federals were enfiladed by that of the Confederate batteries on little Kennesaw, some of the guns of which General French had rolled back from facing north, and turned upon them. This tempest of bombshells, grape and canister, within a short time, drove them back, and relieved Walker from the attack.

An exciting episode of the battle here occurred when a schrapnel shot, with a smoking fuse, passed under the headlog, and fell among the men in the ditch. A stampede instantly commenced, in the midst of which a Georgia sergeant leaped forward, seized the projectile, and threw it out of the trenches, where the explosion did no harm.

But the most determined and powerful assault was made by Palmer's corps of the Army of the Cumberland, with Hooker in reserve, and with such other support as could be spared, upon the intrenchments held by Cheatham's and Cleburne's divisions, which extended through the rolling country south of the mountain. The Federal troops, several lines deep, conscious of their very decided superiority in numbers, pressed forward, with bayonets glistening and banners waving, and with wild cheers, through the forest, which was badly tangled with undergrowth, until they came almost to the Confederate fortifications.

Here an appalling fire was opened upon them from all along the works. By Cleburne's troops, particularly, they were permitted to approach within nearly twenty paces before a gun was fired. Then, there burst forth from beneath the headlogs a fearful sheet of flame and smoke, and, at one or two points, almost the entire Federal column was prostrated by the volley.

Succeeding this murderous sweep of death, there arose from behind the intrenchments a wild and piercing sound. It was the "rebel yell." Often, ere this, had it been heard on the fields of strife; but never before had it smote the ears of those whom it now greeted with more daring defiance than in this minute of horror and blood. Above the roar of battle, clear and shrill, it rang out, and again and yet again was it reechoed from the mountain crags back to the woody recesses of the plain.

Like an inspiration from the genii of ruin, it seemed to arouse those from whose throats it leaped forth, to more than mortal energy; and now, from ten thousand muskets, and from a score of cannon there poured forth an incessant blaze, which scattered carnage and death for hundreds of yards around.

This storm of missiles from the earthworks in front was so destructive that further advance was impossible. The ground and the forest were torn up by musket balls, grape and canister, solid shot, and exploding bombs. From French's batteries on the crest of Kennesaw, also, a furious bombardment was directed upon them. So continuous and rapid was this that the mountain seemed literally on fire; and the murky clouds of smoke, enveloping its summit, and rising majestically toward the heavens, combined with the tumultuous roar from their midst, presented, in terrific grandeur, the veritable appearance of a volcanic eruption; while the air, above and around the assaulting columns, was obscured by the puffs of smoke from the bursting shells, which hurled their fragments in a thousand directions among the Federal ranks, or, screaming through the forest, tore whole trees to pieces, scattering the branches with swaths of destruction on every side.

The Federal troops, dreadfully scourged, lay down upon the ground, within range of the murderous musketry fire of their enemy, and sought all the shelter possible, in the meantime pouring back volley after volley in return; and finally intrenched themselves beneath this fearful tempest — it being safer to remain than to flee.

Once, under General Harker's leadership, they attempted to renew the assault; but, almost at the very parapet, Harker fell, mortally wounded, and the whole line was swept back before the awful iron hail which was poured into their faces. At one or two points the charging columns pressed forward to the very ditches before the breastworks, and some of their dead were found against the works themselves.

The fall of General Harker was greatly deplored by officers and men alike. Gallant, dashing and generous, he had conspicuously distinguished himself on every field of battle from Chickamauga to Kennesaw inclusive; and, of all the field officers in the Federal army, was probably more admired for plucky courage, and more highly esteemed for genial, sociable personal traits, than any of his comrade leaders.

In the midst of the *mêlée* attending this last dash, a United States flag was planted on Cheatham's works. A Confederate captain instantly sprang to the top to gain possession of this. The Federal color-bearer faced him bravely, and a hand-to-hand struggle ensued between the two over the flag, which resulted in the Tennessean's being shot dead by his antagonist. But the next instant a dozen bullets, fired from within the intrenchments, riddled the intrepid color-bearer, and he fell, slain, with his hand tightly clasped around the staff of the banner he had defended so well; but which now became the trophy of the exultant Confederates.

Near this same point a Confederate sergeant leaped over the works, seized the standard of the 27th Illinois regiment, wrested it from the bearer, and brought it triumphantly back with him. For this daring act General Hardee presented the flag to its captor.

Just after the repulse of this second desperate assault, the dry leaves, etc., in the forest, before the Confederate intrenchments, were set on fire by the bombshells and gun-wadding, and began burning rapidly around the Federal wounded. This horrible scene was observed by the Confederates, who were ordered instantly to cease firing, and one of their commanders called to the Federals, and stated that, as an act of humanity, his men would suspend further battle until the assailants could carry off their wounded, who were in danger of being burnt alive. The offer was accepted, and the Federal wounded were rescued from the awful fate which threatened them; and then the combat was renewed by the two sides with the most determined zeal.

In the meantime, along the entire line for miles, there was maintained between both armies a tremendous fire of artillery and musketry. From the crest of Kennesaw Mountain, this is said to have presented an imposing panorama. General French says of it:

"We sat there, perhaps an hour, enjoying a bird's-eye view of one of the most magnificent sights ever allotted to man — to look down upon an hundred and fifty thousand men arrayed in the strife of battle on the plain below. As the infantry chased in the blue smoke of the musket marked out our line for miles, while over it, rose in cumuli-like clouds the white smoke of the artillery. Through the rifts of smoke, or, as it was wafted aside by the wind, we could see the assault made on Cheatham, and there the struggle was hard, and there it lasted longest. So many guns were trained on those by our side, and so incessant was the roar of cannon and the sharp explosion of shells, that naught else could be heard.   *   *   The battle, in its entirety, became a pageantry on a grand scale, and barren of results, because the attacking columns were too small in numbers, considering the character of the troops they knew they would encounter."

In this great struggle the Federal army numbered about or over 100,000 men, the Confederates had about 55,000 engaged; the Confederate loss, in killed, wounded and missing, was 808 men; that of the Federals has never been exactly reported, but it is conceded that it went up into the thousands.

Sherman's generals, after some three hours, withdrew their shattered battalions from nearly all the points of assault, and, for one time, there was a confessed failure of a great move in the campaign.

But wasting no time in idle regrets, the Federal commander ordered a strong movement down the valley of Olley's Creek, toward the Chattahoochee.

June 29th, he wired General Halleck in reference to this: " I am accumulating stores that will enable me to cut loose from the railroad for a time and avoid the Kennesaw Hill, which gives the enemy too much advantage."

July 1st, he again wired him: " By this movement, I think I can force Johnston to move his whole army out from Kennesaw to defend his railroad and the Chattahoochee, when I will (by the left flank) reach the railroad below Marietta."

Johnston, however, seeing that this movement towards the south would result in breaking his communications with Atlanta, evacuated Kennesaw Mountain and Marietta during the 1st and 2d of July, the last columns withdrawing in the night of the latter.

While the evacuation was going on, under General Johnston's orders, a terrific bombardment of the Federal positions was maintained from the batteries on the crest of the mountain, with the idea of distracting the attention of the Federals, and leading to the belief that possibly a sortie was contemplated from some portion of the Confederate lines.

During the afternoon of July 2d, the Confederates withdrew their guns from Kennesaw Mountain. Major Storrs, of General French's command, who was in partial charge, describes this feat as follows:

" It had been predicted that our batteries could not be safely withdrawn in case of retreat. An order came one day to remove them between sundown and dark; or else spike the guns and destroy the carriages. Routes were trimmed out straight down immediately in rear of each section, and every gun arrived at the base of the mountain by dark, without attracting a single shot from the enemy. We had been keeping our embrasures covered with brush to conceal our movements when preparing to deliver a shot, so that everything was hidden. On the left, the upper part of a man's body while standing, could be seen by the enemy, and so Lieutenants Harris and Murphy, of Gailoes battery, with their men, crawled on their hands and knees while withdrawing the left section and lowered those two pieces over a declivity by means of ropes."

From Marietta, Johnston fell back to a new position, which had been prepared by Colonel Prestman. This consisted of what General Sherman calls one of the strongest pieces of field fortification he ever saw. It ran from the Chattahoochee River, south of the Western & Atlantic Railroad, up through the hill country, across it, thence joining the river again some two or three miles above, its entire length being several miles.

Sherman thought that in the hurry of evacuation Johnston's army would be in considerable confusion; hence, pressed his columns forward with great energy, to crush the Confederates, if possible; but it was soon demonstrated that Johnston had prepared against this very contingency by throwing up a long east and west line of intrenchments, which crossed the railroad at Ruff's Station, and also another, crossing it at Smyrna. These delayed the Federals so very much that the pursuit accomplished nothing in the results Sherman wished.

MAP OF ATLANTA

Sherman's opinion of Johnston's shrewdness and forethought in this matter was expressed in a dispatch, wherein he said: "We ought to have caught Johnston on his retreat, but he had prepared the way too well."

There was a sharp fight at the works at Ruff's, July 3d; and the 4th of July was celebrated by quite a struggle at the intrenchments at Smyrna, in which the Federals were repulsed. General Noyes of Ohio here lost his leg, and General Sherman says: "I came very near being shot myself." The Federals, however, made a strong demonstration against the line near the Chattahoochee; but, being met by a heavy fire, were compelled to draw off.

During the next few days, with a strong array confronting the Confederate fortifications, several columns were also thrown out by Sherman, north and south of Johnston's position, for a number of miles each way, which resulted in securing the possession of one or two crossings over the Chattahoochee. Accordingly, after some fighting at several points, Johnston evacuated this position, and crossed the Chattahoochee River, burning the railroad bridge.

The two armies, now almost in the suburbs of Atlanta, began preparing for what would have been a tedious siege, when, on the 17th of July, General Johnston was relieved of the command of the army, and General Hood appointed to succeed him.

This change of commanders by the Confederate government amounted to a change of programme; and Sherman, being almost intuitively aware of it, changed his tactics accordingly, and, instead of assaulting or making offensive movements against the Confederate lines, assumed a strong position on Peachtree Creek, northward of Atlanta.

On the 20th of July, General Hood made an impetuous assault upon the Federal army; but the Confederates were worsted in the battle, and sustained considerable loss.

The heavy battle of the 22d of July, between Atlanta and Decatur, in which General McPherson and the Confederate General Walker were killed, gained no advantage to the Confederates; nor did the battle of Ezra Church, on the 28th of July.

The mistake which was made in removing the prudent and sagacious Johnston, and abandoning his Fabian tactics, substituting therefor an aggressive policy by an army which had scarcely more than half its enemy's numbers, is one which, in the present day, finds almost no one to defend it.

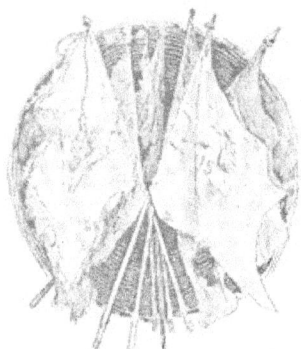

> " But turn the page, let War's dread name
>   Be buried with his dead;
> O'er every scar let peaceful Fame
>   Her downy mantle spread;
> Beat into useful plowshares now
>   The once blood-dripping sword,
> And from each council-chamber vow
>   To banish fierce discord !"

So let us cease the recital of the deeds of strife and of ruin, which, over twenty years ago, were enacted with the thunder of cannon, the waving of banners, and all the "gorgeous panoply of war," amid the craggy mountains, and forest-covered hills and valleys, and by the rushing rivers of North Georgia. High in the Temple of Fame glitter the names of Chickamauga, Ringgold, Resaca, Allatoona, Kennesaw Mountain and Atlanta, and of the heroes, who, around them, fought for their Union, their cause, and their flag. Whether mistaken or true were their teachings let us presume not to judge. Sufficient it is that over two hundred thousand men, upon these fields of carnage, bared their breasts to sustain their convictions, and eighty-eight thousand shed their blood in defence of what they thought was right.

The long struggle is ended; the wail of humiliation is hushed, and the huzza of proud triumph is over; the cypress has draped the coffins of the vanquished, and the laurel has crowned the victor's brow.